WE BOTH READ™

Parent's Introduction

We Both Read is the first series of books designed to invite parents and children to share the reading of a story by taking turns reading aloud. This "shared reading" innovation, which was developed in conjunction with early reading specialists, invites parents to read the more sophisticated text on the left-hand pages, while children are encouraged to read the right-hand pages, which have been written at one of three early reading levels.

Reading aloud is one of the most important activities parents can share with their child to assist their reading development. However, *We Both Read* goes beyond reading *to* a child and allows parents to share reading *with* a child. *We Both Read* is so powerful and effective because it combines two key elements in learning: "showing" (the parent reads) and "doing" (the child reads). The result is not only faster reading development for the child, but a much more enjoyable and enriching experience for both!

Most of the words used in the child's text should be familiar to them. Others can easily be sounded out. An occasional difficult word will be first introduced in the parent's text, distinguished with **bold lettering**. Pointing out these words, as you read them, will help familiarize them to your child. You may also find it helpful to read the entire book aloud yourself the first time, then invite your child to participate on the second reading. Also note that the parent's text is preceded by a "talking parent" icon: ; and the child's text is preceded by a "talking child" icon: .

We Both Read books is a fun, easy way to encourage and help your child to read — and a wonderful way to start your child off on a lifetime of reading enjoyment!

We Both Read: About Bugs

Use of photographs provided by Dr. Edward Ross and Animals Animals/
Richard Kolar, Patti Murray, Donald Specker, Ken G. Preston-Mafham,
Michael Fogden, James H. Robinson, Stephen Dalton, Michael Andrews,
Doug Wechsler, G. I. Bernard, O. S. F., Raymond A. Mendez,
Bruce Davidson, Richard La Val.

We Both Read™ is a trademark of Treasure Bay, Inc.

Published by Treasure Bay, Inc.
50 Horgan Ave., Suite 12
Redwood City, CA 94061 USA

PRINTED IN SINGAPORE

Library of Congress Catalog Card Number: 98-60701
Hardcover ISBN 1-891327-07-0
Softcover ISBN 1-891327-11-9

FIRST EDITION

We Both Read™ Books
Patent Pending

WE BOTH READ™

About
Bugs

By
Sheryl Scarborough

TREASURE BAY

Ladybug swarm

Does it sometimes seem like bugs are everywhere? Well, they *are*!

There are more bugs in the world than there are people and all other animals combined. And different kinds of bugs can live in almost any weather condition, from extreme heat to freezing cold.

Bugs, or **insects**, are some of the strangest and most mysterious creatures alive. But just what is a bug?

Head   Thorax   Abdomen

Red ant

The real name for a bug is "**insect**."

The body of an insect has three parts.

All insects have six legs.

Spiders are *not* insects.

Spiders have eight legs.

Giraffe beetle

One kind of insect is the **beetle**. There are over 500,000 species of **beetle**, each with its own unique characteristics. The bombardier **beetle**, for example, turns the lower part of its body into a powerful cannon to shoot its attacker with a cloud of foul smelling hot gas.

The **beetle** shown above is called the giraffe **beetle**. Can you guess why?

Hercules beetle

Beetles come in all shapes and sizes.
Some beetles are good. They eat other bugs.
Some beetles are bad. They eat plants, trees,
and even rugs!

Honeybee with stinger extended

Every **honeybee** hive has one queen that is in charge of the hive and will produce all the offspring. Each spring she sends her workers out to gather **pollen** and **nectar**. The bees then convert the **nectar** into honey, which will be stored for food.

Worker bees use their stingers to protect the hive's honey from marauding animals — including humans!

Honeybee in flight

The **honeybees** gather **pollen** and **nectar**
from flowers.
They gather the pollen with their back legs.
Then they fly back to the hive with this food.

Praying mantis

Mantids are often called praying mantises because the position of their front legs gives the impression they are praying.

Mantids have a voracious appetite and will eat just about any bug they can grab with their trap-like front legs. They will sit very still until another insect approaches, then grab it and eat it alive!

Leaf-like mantid

There are many kinds of **mantids**. Some are hard to see when they are on a plant. This helps mantids hide from animals that eat bugs. This one looks like a leaf.

Giant weta

The New Zealand **weta**, which is close to extinction, lives on protected islands near New Zealand. This is one of the largest insects known and can weigh as much as a small bird. Its scientific name — *Deinacrida* — means demon grasshopper because it looks like a large, armor-plated grasshopper.

Wellington tree weta

The **weta** lives in a hole in the ground.

It only comes out at night.

The weta's ears are on its legs.

Can you find them?

Mosquito sucking blood

Mosquitoes are often called the vampires of the bug world. Female **mosquitoes** (the only ones that "bite") actually pierce your skin with a pointed appendage called a stylet, then suck blood up one side of the stylet while injecting saliva into your skin with the other side. It's the saliva that makes you itch!

Mosquito larvae and pupa

Mosquitoes lay their eggs in water.
Young mosquitoes find food in the water.
Mosquitoes stay near water until they are
old enough to fly away.

Rabbit flea on rabbit ear

Another blood-sucking member of the insect world is the **flea**. These tiny bugs are only about the size of a pinhead, but they can deliver a very big "itch!"

The small, flat, slippery body of the **flea** allows it to slide easily through the hairs or feathers of its involuntary "host."

Cat flea jumping

A **flea** has strong back legs that help it jump.

A flea can jump very high.

It can jump from the ground up to your knees.

That's a big jump for a little flea!

Spicebush swallowtail caterpillar

A **caterpillar** starts out inching its way through life, but soon blooms into a splendid **butterfly** or **moth** — if it survives.

Fortunately each variety of **caterpillar** has a special way of protecting itself from predators. The spicebush swallowtail **caterpillar** shown here bears a natural disguise to trick its enemies into thinking it's a snake!

Moth Caterpillar shedding skin

A **caterpillar's** skin does not grow. It breaks open when it gets too tight. Then the caterpillar crawls out in a new soft skin. This happens many times before it becomes a **butterfly** or **moth**.

Atlas moth

The variety of caterpillars is vast. But eventually most will spin a cocoon or form a chrysalis from which they will emerge as moths or butterflies in a multitude of sizes and colors.

The largest moths and butterflies live in the tropics. Some, like this Atlas moth, can have a wingspan of eleven inches.

Spicebush swallowtail butterfly

Is it a butterfly or a moth? How can you tell?

Most moths fly at night.

All butterflies fly in the day.

A moth rests with its wings out.

A butterfly rests with its wings up.

Honey pot ants

There are over 8,000 different kinds, or species, of ant, each with its own fascinating method of survival.

Some are fierce hunters. Some harvest and store seeds. Honey pot ants use some of the ants in their colony as living storage containers to hold sweet juice for the winter or a dry season.

One of the most interesting species of ant is the army ant. **African army ants** live in the **jungles** of Africa in large **groups** or colonies.

Army ants attacking katydid

African army ants march through the **jungle**.
They march in big **groups**.
They eat almost any small animal in their path.
But even *big* animals can be scared of African
army ants!

Tarantula hawk wasp and tarantula

The tarantula hawk **wasp** is one of the most fascinating species in the **wasp** family. This **wasp** will inject a tarantula spider with a paralyzing venom, then lay a single egg on its warm, furry back. The **wasp's** resulting larva then feeds on the immobilized spider until it's strong enough to be on its own.

Social wasps on a nest

There are many different kinds of **wasps**. Some wasps make paper to build their nests. People may have learned how to make paper by watching these wasps!

Assassin bug piercing grasshopper head

Assassin bugs are some of the insect world's most impressive predators and each of the hundreds of species hunt, kill, and feed in a similar way.

Most wait quietly in hiding to surprise their victim, then use their dagger-like beak to kill their prey. This same beak also serves as a feeding tube for the **assassin** bug.

Assassin bug nymph

Some **assassin** bugs live near people.
Sometimes assassin bugs bite people.
It hurts when they bite!
But the bite does not kill people.

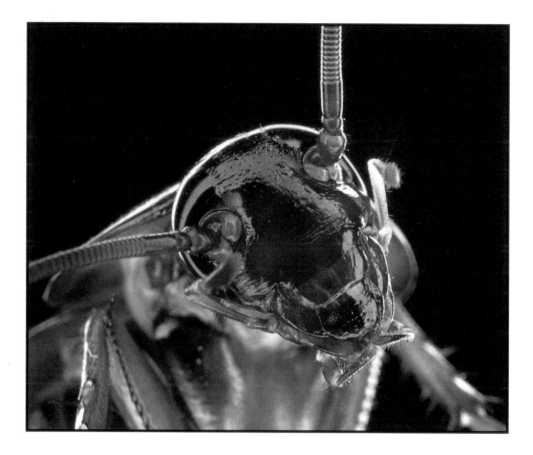

American cockroach head

Many people think **cockroaches** are nasty, dirty creatures, but these bugs actually clean themselves as often as cats.

Cockroaches roamed Earth before the dinosaurs and are so adaptable to their environment they will probably continue to roam for a long time to come.

Giant cockroach

A **cockroach** can be as small as an ant.

Some can be as big as a mouse.

This one is a called a "Giant Cockroach."

It can grow up to 6 inches long!

Southern aeshna dragonfly

The wings of the brightly colored **dragonfly** seem fragile but are actually such powerful and efficient flight organs that the U.S. military studied them to try and make their planes fly faster.

A **dragonfly's** head can move in many directions and is almost all eye. This allows **dragonflies** to see prey up to 40 feet away. Then they swoop in to nab the prey right out of the air.

Red dragonfly on sisal leaf

Dragonflies have been on Earth a long time. They were on Earth before the dinosaurs. Back then a dragonfly was longer than your arm. Now a dragonfly is about as long as your hand.

Fulgora (lantern bug) head

This odd looking bug with a head shaped like a peanut is found in the tropical regions of Central and South America. Fulgora, which means "bright light" in Latin, is also called a **lantern** bug because it was once thought to produce light.

The fulgora's "peanut head" is a form of protection, making it look like a lizard to an attacking **enemy**.

Fulgora (lantern bug) with wings extended

Lantern bugs spread their wings when an
enemy comes near. Spots on the lantern
bug's wings look like the eyes of an owl.
This is another way to scare an enemy away.

Two walking sticks

Walking sticks look just like the twigs of the trees in which they live. This natural camouflage makes them appear to be something inedible to birds, their main enemies.

Walking sticks are greedy leaf-eating vegetarians who do most of their eating at night when the birds are asleep.

Dead leaf butterfly

A **walking stick** stays safe by not being seen.
Many bugs stay safe this way.
This butterfly looks like a dead leaf.

Queen, worker and soldier termites

Unfortunately for humans, **termites** are found in almost every part of the world that humans inhabit. These little bugs eat wood and paper at an amazing rate and can cause lots of damage to houses and other structures.

Termites live in colonies under the rule of a queen who lays all the eggs and is cared for by the worker **termites**.

Gigantic termite nest

Some **termites** live in nests.

Some termite nests can be taller than a person!

Some people in Africa use mud from these nests to make walls for their huts.

Katydid from Florida

Katy-did-katy-did! That's the beautiful love call of the **katydid**.

Katydids make their distinctive sounds, often called their song, by rubbing the base of their front wings together. Many start their song at twilight and sing through the entire night, hoping to attract a mate.

Katydid from Ecuador

 Katydids live where it is warm.

Most katydids live in trees and bushes.

This katydid is from South America.

Goliath beetle

There are over one million different known species of bugs in the world. Here are some fun facts about some of them.

One of the smallest known insects is the hummingbird flower mite. It lives in the nose of a hummingbird!

One of the heaviest flying insects is the 5" long, massively armored goliath beetle of Africa.

Hawk moth

One of the fastest running bugs is the cockroach.

It can run 60 feet per minute.

One of the fastest flying bugs is the hawk moth.

It can fly up to 33 miles per hour.

Weta-like katydid

Insects appear in an almost infinite variety of shapes, sizes and colors. Some have no ears or noses on their faces yet can smell and hear better than humans. Some have two wings, some have four, and some have no wings at all.

People called entomologists spend their whole lives in the study of these fascinating creatures we call bugs.

Scarab beetle taking flight

Would you like to study bugs?

You can start in your own yard!

Bugs are everywhere.

How many different kinds can you find?